GAME NIGHT

by Adam Hannigan

Published by Playdead Press 2023

A CIP catalogue record for this book is available from the British Library.

ISBN 978-1-915533-07-4

Playdead Press
www.playdeadpress.com

This production of *Game Night* was performed with the following cast and creative:

CAST

MICHAEL	**Adam Hannigan**
JACOB	**James Sinclair**
KATE	**Amelie Rose**
TOM	**Jimmy Jameson**
CLAIRE	**Tiffany Robinson**
RORY	**Ryan McGonagle**
SHANE	**James Colebrook**

CREATIVE TEAM

Writer, Director, Producer	**Adam Hannigan**
Producer, Assistant Director	**Jenson Parker Stone**
Producer, Design	**Amy Brown**
Producer	**Tiffany Robinson**
Illustrator, Artistic Design	**Jimmy Doodle**
Tech Design	**Dickson Cossar/ Hannah Ellaway**

SPECIAL THANKS

Zina Cochrane

Jess Carrivick

Blair Gibson

Ear to Ear Productions

Ear to Ear Productions is a theatre company based in London, established in September 2014, by three final year (Acting for Stage and Media) students.

Our work is light-hearted and comical, whilst addressing real people in real situations. The underlining themes address self-acceptance with sexuality and within society.

We are currently trying to broaden our following and will be touring our current pieces round fringes and other venues.

We celebrate the diversity of life and the LGBTQ+ community.

The name Ear to Ear Productions originated as a symbol of smiling which sums up the ethos and the goal of our company.

We make sure to offer something for everyone.

Instagram:	@eartoearprod / @gamenightuk
Twitter:	@eartoearprod / @gamenightuk
Website:	eartoearproduction.wixsite.com/theatre
Facebook:	Ear to Ear Productions

THANKS & DEDICATIONS

I want to thank all my family, friends and everyone who has supported me this far in my career, anyone who has taken a chance on me and my work, anyone who donated their time or money *(or both)* to help me reach my goals. I also want to thank *Playdead Press* for making this all possible. Lastly and most importantly I want to thank everyone in my team at *Ear to Ear Productions* and the amazing cast of Game Night *(past and present)* for believing in my story and helping to bring it to life, I couldn't have done this without you all.

Dedicated to D & P.

WRITERS NOTE

I am a 29 year old gay actor and writer living in London. I come from a little town in Northern Ireland which is why people can never understand anything I say. I moved to London to pursue my passion for acting and writing but in this current economy I am also desperately considering porn to pay for the fancy lifestyle I want to live.

I love getting involved with fresh projects, challenging myself whilst learning all aspects of the industry, apart from dance... I can give it a go if you'd like but don't expect much. I created *Ear to Ear Productions* in my final year of university aiming my work to be a sense of escapism and acceptance for the queer community, doing so through slapstick comedy and satire. My biggest influences are noughties sitcoms such as '*Friends*' and '*Will & Grace*'. Ironically, I first got interested in the industry at a very young age when I watched the iconic horror movie '*Scream*'. I loved how it perfectly balanced horror and humour in such a camp yet self-aware way and it truly inspired me. Kevin Williamson is my writing inspiration so if anyone knows him get me in touch, please. I also love cats and will try to find a way to involve them in any project I work on.

Game Night was an idea that came to me in 2017. My favourite kind of comedic dramas are situational events when all characters are forced together under mundane circumstances and things unravel. I originally wrote the role of Rory for myself, as he was very much my casting but then decided I wanted to 'challenge' myself and play Michael. When creating the role of Michael, I found him to be very irritating and high maintenance, so it was great when many people laughed and said how he reminded them of me. When writing and directing the play, it was important to me that all these characters, no matter how eccentric where grounded and 'real'. It was also very important that we never exploited any of the queer communities' traumas and created an honest look into the lives of the queer community but of course in a comedic manner. The best thing in the world is to make people laugh.

If you want to get in touch or give me a job, follow me!

Instagram: @adamhango

Twitter: @adamhango

If you like my style and my ethos check out my other company '*Insecure Unicorn*' where me and my friend interview members of the queer community and share their stories.

Instagram: @thetinsecureunicornteam

Twitter: @insecureunicorn

Adam Hannigan

ACT 1

Italicized dialogue beginning with '' is open for modification to modern pop culture and current affairs.*

[Int. Fade up on a cozy dining room.]

[Enter MICHAEL who is setting the room and getting ready.]

MICHAEL: *(Looking in the mirror)* I'm engaged! Ok, less enthusiasm. *(Emotionless)* I'm engaged. No, umm let's make it fun? *(Dancing)* Guess who's enga... stop it. Ok, just slip it into conversation, just casually slip it in: "Did you guys hear about Donna? Yeah she was stabbed 37 times... I'm engaged." Come on just make it real! Guys, I'm engaged.

[JACOB has been watching from the door.]

JACOB: Don't you mean *we* are engaged?

MICHAEL: What?

JACOB: You said *you* were engaged but shouldn't you be saying *we*?

MICHAEL: Right. *(Pause)* Look I want to say that I will work on it but I'm pretty much set in my ways.

JACOB: Right.

[Michael begins re-organising the pillows on the sofa.]

MICHAEL: Thanks for doing this tonight, by the way. I know I've been driving you crazy with my obsessive need to make everything perfect, but when it comes down to it, really all that matters to me is… is that, that's not the top I picked out for you.

JACOB: Oh yeah, I just like this one better; I feel more relaxed in it.

MICHAEL: Ok, first of all, stop shouting at me, and secondly, sweetie, this is our pre-engagement party *party*, ok? You're lucky I'm not making you wear a tuxedo.

JACOB: Yeah but its only game night, so I just thought I'd – *(noticing Michael's face, without hesitation)* quickly go change.

[Jacob kisses Michael on the cheek and leaves.]

MICHAEL: Ok! But only if *you* want to, though. Oh, my god, I almost had to call off the entire wedding. Ok! Something's missing. *(Looks around getting into a panic)* wine! I'm Irish, how could I forget the alcohol? Oh, where did I put those bottles? *(Panics)*

[Enter Jacob carrying bottles of wine.]

JACOB: They're right here. *(Laughing)* Michael, relax.

MICHAEL: I am relaxed. I just want it all to be perfect.

JACOB: I'm sure it will be, but aren't they going to notice the ring right away, anyway?

MICHAEL: Well, no, because it's really small. I'm joking, besides, have you met my friends? They are so self-indulgent they wouldn't even notice if we had engagement banners leading up to the front door.

JACOB: Well, they can be…

MICHAEL: I once saw Kate use a car side mirror to fix her makeup.

JACOB: How does that make her self-indulgent?

MICHAEL: It was during a car crash Jacob. People died. A lot of people.

JACOB: Well then why go to all this trouble?

MICHAEL: I don't know, it's more for us than it is for them. I just thought it would be nice for us to look back on tonight and think of how great it was when we told everyone. You know, they all think it's an average game night, then we surprise them? We would all have a toast, Rory would get too drunk as usual, you and I would win the games as usual, and Kate and Tom would go home feeling like their relationship just isn't as good as ours… as usual, it would be perfect.

JACOB: Wow. All that pre-planned fun. Sounds great.

MICHAEL: And we can just take that comment and put it on the shelf for a later date. I'm gonna get the games.

[As Michael leaves, Jacob can be seen adding 2 extras wine glasses to the table. He grows nervous.]

JACOB: He is going to kill me.

MICHAEL: *(Offstage)* Are we thinking charades or something more like poker?

JACOB: I'd say poker.

[Michael enters carrying Charades.]

MICHAEL: So, I decided on charades. Don't give me that look I just think it gives a more upbeat vibe to the night. Don't you agree?

JACOB: Isn't it a bit childish?

MICHAEL: Well, I'm glad that's settled. Ok, so let's go over it one more time.

JACOB: Michael, we've gone over it like ten times today alone.

MICHAEL: I know but still... So, when everyone is getting a little bored of the games, I will give you the signal and you go get the champagne and I will get everyone's attention. Then once we tell them the news, I will ask Rory and Kate to be my maid and gay of honour.

JACOB: You do realise that's not a plan? You are just saying when people get bored of our party let's give them more drink, so they forget and put all their attention on you. Michael?

[Michael is in a daze of self-appraisal.]

JACOB: Michael? *(Snaps fingers)* Michael!

MICHAEL: What's your point?

[Jacob smirks and pulls Michael closer.]

MICHAEL: [Cont'd] You said you were happy to tell them this way. If it makes you feel uncomfortable at all, we can cancel the whole thing.

JACOB: Michael I don't care how we tell them, it's not the announcement I care about

[They kiss.]

MICHAEL: Oh, thank God because they are already on their way so we can't really cancel anything.

JACOB: Hmm love you too.

MICHAEL: Oh, shut up! You know I love you, why else would I marry you?

JACOB: Umm maybe for my amazing, good looks?

MICHAEL: Jacob I'm trying to have a serious moment here.

JACOB: Fuck you.

[Jacob throws a pillow at Michael.]

MICHAEL: I'm joking! Now who needs to relax? *(Begins massaging Jacob's shoulders)* You're right though, everything is going to be fine and we both just need to take a breath and just relax. But before you do, why don't you go grab the brownies from the kitchen? I'm trying out a new recipe for the café.

JACOB: Is that what smells so good?

MICHAEL: *(Aggressively grabbing his shoulders)* Touch one before they arrive, and I'll break your fucking hand! *(Jumping back)* Can't wait to get married.

[Michael goes to leave.]

JACOB: So, did you do it?

MICHAEL: Do what?

JACOB: Tell your parents about the wedding?

MICHAEL: Oh, it's actually a really funny story! So, I was going to but then… I didn't.

JACOB: You have to tell them soon Michael, what if they hear it from Rory or Rory's mum?

MICHAEL: Well then Rory's mum can deal with their disappointment.

JACOB: Michael, you need to…

MICHAEL: Look, it's easier for you! Your mum loves her big gay son!

JACOB: Ok, yeah, fair, my family are more open than yours, but still, you will regret it if you don't tell them. Imagine not having your parents being there on our wedding day. I know you. You would hate that.

[Silence.]

MICHAEL: You don't know me.

JACOB: Well, I know I'd hate it if my family weren't there.

MICHAEL: I mean I wouldn't mind if your sister wasn't there.

JACOB: Michael.

MICHAEL: I know, I know I will put fifty P in the 'your sister's a bitch' jar.

JACOB: You know, I'm really not ok with you having that jar.

MICHAEL: And yet you liked the watch it paid for on your birthday.

JACOB: What?

MICHAEL: **Nothing. So, what did Hagrid say when you told her we are getting married?*

JACOB: *(Awkward)* Oh. I... I umm, I haven't told her yet. I'm seeing her this weekend so I will tell her then.

MICHAEL: God, good luck with that.

JACOB: I'm sure she will be fine.

MICHAEL: Yeah, because she has always been so accepting of me.

JACOB: She has?

MICHAEL: Jacob, she bought me a book on how to be single in the city.

JACOB: Well, you know, that can be…

MICHAEL: It was for our four-year Anniversary.

JACOB: Oh, it was probably a joke.

MICHAEL: Yeah, and the time she made me try lobster without telling me what it was, and I almost died was probably just a silly prank.

JACOB: She didn't know you were allergic to shellfish.

MICHAEL: Her exact words where "Try this, Michael, it doesn't contain any shellfish in it what-so-ever'.

JACOB: I'm sure there must be some mis-understanding, maybe she…

[Doorbell rings.]

MICHAEL: Oh, my god, that's them! I'm not ready! It's open! Ahh! Quick, act natural.

[Michael awkwardly poses.]

JACOB: What are you doing?

MICHAEL: What are you doing? We need to stall them! We're in the living room! Dammit!

[Michael prances around panicking.]

JACOB: Michael, calm down! Everything is going to be fine, and your friends are going to be so happy and excited for you.

MICHAEL: Are you sure?

JACOB: Yes, because they're kind and caring people.

[KATE & TOM storm in.]

KATE: I hope your dick falls off!

TOM: I hope your cunt dries up!

[They all stop and awkwardly smile.]

KATE / TOM: Hello.

MICHAEL / JACOB: Guys.

JACOB: How are y…

[Kate throws her coat over Jacob's face and storms to the sofa. Tom throws he bag over Jacob's open arms and follows her.]

MICHAEL: Guys, is everything ok?

KATE: Oh, it's nothing, don't worry about it.

TOM: Yeah, just typical married coupled stuff. Typical frigid stuff.

KATE: Oh, Tom sweetie, when you smile like that you always remind me of someone.

TOM: A prince?

KATE: Yeh, Prince Andrew

TOM: I guess that makes you the Duchess of Pork.

KATE: Oh, I'm sorry I've not had time to work out with cleaning up after you every day as if I'm your mother.

TOM: Don't make this about my mother again.

KATE: Fuck your mother!

TOM: You wish you could fuck my mother!

KATE: No one wishes they could fuck your mother, that's why your dad killed himself!

TOM: Cancer killed my dad!

KATE: He let the cancer kill him!

[Long awkward silence.]

JACOB: Ok, I'm just gonna grab those snacks.

[Jacob exits.]

MICHAEL: So... did you guys get here ok with that storm?

KATE: Oh, yeh it was fine. It actually reminded me of the time the doctor told us that Tom was shooting blanks.

MICHAEL: I don't think my question really set up that answer, but ok.

TOM: I think what Kate was trying to say was that she is a suffocating narcissist who is too lazy to make other people happy.

[They both stand to approach one another when Michael jumps to his feet.]

MICHAEL: Wine! Who wants wine?

[He pours them a glass as they all sit down. An awkward silence follows. Kate & Tom loudly sip their drinks.]

So, how are you guys?

KATE: Ok.

TOM: Fine.

KATE: Good.

TOM: Great.

KATE: Fantastic.

TOM: Ecstatic.

KATE: Betrayed!

TOM: Untouched!

MICHAEL: I'm just gonna keep filling these glasses right up to the top.

[Jacob enters.]

JACOB: So, rumor has it from the kitchen everyone is feeling great?

MICHAEL: Please don't leave again.

KATE: So, Jacob how is the new job going?

JACOB: Really well, yeh we...

KATE: Tom quit his job. Yeah, he felt like it wasn't satisfying enough for him, which is a common thing for him at the moment. He said he wants to focus on professional golf, so you know we will be rolling in it any day now.

TOM: At least I'm passionate about something in my life.

KATE: Yeah, we will make sure to put that on your gravestone: "He didn't achieve much but was passionate about it".

MICHAEL: Look, is everything ok? You both seem a bit tense.

KATE: **Hmm, the only tension I've noticed is Tom's hand around yet another mega pint of wine.*

TOM: **Oh, pipe down Amber heard!*

JACOB: *(To Michael)* You've made it worse.

KATE: It's like this Michael, you know sometimes when you buy a really colourful top, but after a few washes the colour fades? Yeah, well Tom is the washing machine and his love for me is the top.

TOM: Does that make you the hot water just sucking the life out of it?

MICHAEL: This isn't really the theme I imagined for the evening.

KATE: I'm sorry, Michael, marriage is just tough. Trust me, you don't know how good you and Jacob have it here: no pressure, no documentation forcing you by law, no watching him stick his hand inside his jeans and scratching his sweaty hairy balls then dipping the same fingers into your low-fat yogurt cause Donna at work asked if you were pregnant and when you said no, she just smiled and said 'good for you'.

TOM: **No smelling her farts that smell like a gay orgy and pretending it was the cat.*

KATE: No picking up his skiddy boxers.

TOM: No blue balls.

KATE: Wait, how do you know what a gay orgy smells like?

[Jacobs phone rings.]

JACOB: Oh, thank God, it's Max. *(Answering)* Hey, Buddy, what's… aww that's amazing. No, don't worry we understand. Yeah, let me know how everything goes. Send our love to Charlie. *(Ends call)* Max's girlfriend just went into labour!

MICHAEL: Great! Now my seating plan is ruined. I mean… yay congratulations. Oh, but we have uneven teams now for charades, we don't have a partner for Rory. Wait, where is Rory? Wasn't he travelling in with you guys?

[RORY storms in looking out of breath.]

RORY: What the hell?

MICHAEL: Where have you been?

RORY: In the car! They locked me in! I had to climb out the sunroof!

KATE: See Tom look what you did!

TOM: You were the one driving.

KATE: Oh, so now I'm a bad driver. Let me guess because I'm a woman?

TOM: Can we not do this here?

KATE: Fine!

MICHAEL: Ok, just ignoring all of that, can I get you a drink, Rory?

RORY: Yes, please! I need it to thaw off from that blizzard I had to crawl through, not to mention being stuck with all you couples for the night.

JACOB: Oh, Rory that reminds me, my friend Max had to cancel so we don't really have a partner for you for charades.

RORY: Couldn't even wait until I had my drink could you, Jacob?

MICHAEL: *(To Rory)* What the hell is going on with these two?

RORY: I don't know, they were going mad at each other in the car so eventually I just put my earphones in and started doing poppers.

MICHAEL: Rory!

RORY: Want some?

MICHAEL: Maybe later.

RORY: Right, let's get this night started. I can't be up too late I have an audition tomorrow morning.

MICHAEL: Ooh, what for?

RORY: Ahh, it's top secret, but it's a pretty big deal.

KATE: Really?

RORY: Let's just say they are providing travel fees *and* lunch so…

KATE: Nice and what's the pay like?

RORY: I *just* told you they are providing travel fees *and* lunch.

TOM: Well, I think it's great you are doing what you love no matter the struggle.

KATE: Suck a tit and die Tom.

RORY: So, why is your friend bailing on me? He a homophobe?

JACOB: No, his girlfriend just went into labour.

RORY: Straight breeding? Even worse.

MICHAEL: Why do you dislike kids so much?

RORY: I don't *dislike* kids. [Beat.] I *hate* kids.

KATE: I love babies they are so cute!

RORY: Yeah, like you would be a good mother, I almost froze to death in the back seat of your car.

[Tom laughs, Kate glares at him.]

KATE: Oh, my god! So how was New York?

MICHAEL: It was amazing! We had the best time, and you should have seen the room. Jacob rang ahead and told them about our anniversary, so they bumped us up to the penthouse suite!

KATE: Shut up!

RORY: Yes, please do.

MICHAEL: Yeah, the view was unbelievable, and they had a bottle of champagne waiting for us with chocolates and complimentary massages!

KATE: That's so good! Tom never does anything like that for me.

TOM: I did that for you last year in France, no? I told Jacob about it!

KATE: That was the honeymoon suite not the penthouse.

TOM: They didn't have a penthouse!

KATE: Full of excuses aren't you!

JACOB: Is that where you proposed?

KATE: Ha!

TOM: Why would you bring that up?

RORY: I forget this story - how did you propose?

JACOB: I don't think I've ever heard it either.

TOM: Well, my plan was to...

KATE: He threw up on me and lost the ring.

TOM: No!

JACOB: How?

KATE: Because he proposed to me on a Ferris wheel, forgetting he was deathly afraid of heights.

TOM: No, let me explain!

KATE: Then he passed out and pissed himself!

JACOB: You peed?

TOM: No! Well yes but... look, yes, I'm afraid of heights but I took Kate to the fun fair on our first date, and she really wanted to go on the Ferris wheel but I chickened out and so I thought it would be nice to finally take her up there and it would be perfect to propose at the top. However, I was so nervous all day that I hadn't ate and when we did get to the top, well, I didn't realise they were going to stop the ride up there for that long. So, I panicked…

KATE: He cried.

TOM: I didn't cry.

KATE: Your penis did.

TOM: I panicked! I had a panic attack.

KATE: When he collapsed, he dropped the ring over the edge, and they never found it.

JACOB: Wow.

RORY: I actually do remember that story I just love making them tell it.

KATE: Anyway, speaking of proposals, how long have you guys been together?

JACOB: Proposal? What proposal?

MICHAEL: Yeah! What's that supposed to mean?

KATE: I was just joking relax. Besides, marriage isn't for everyone… *(Glares at Tom)* trust me. How long have you been together though? Five years?

JACOB: Well technically six but the first year was kinda… well?

RORY: You were fuck buddies, just say it.

JACOB: Well, I was gonna say openly dating.

RORY: Yeah, open is the main word cause Michael and me were hitting that sauna every Monday night.

JACOB: Oh, really?

RORY: Do you remember that night on the swing?

MICHAEL: Ah, so how about you, Rory? Dating anyone these days?

RORY: Oh, some here some there, y'know... I was seeing this guy from Brazil for a bit.

KATE: Oh, what's he called?

RORY: **Oh, no, with Grindr hook-ups you don't use names, or condoms! Ahh I'm a slut!*

KATE: Classy Gays.

RORY: **Shit that reminds me I forgot to take my PrEP again!*

JACOB: So, a swing huh?

MICHAEL: We have guests.

RORY: Basically, we were in the sauna, and there was this swing and I found Michael...

MICHAEL: Rory let's not talk about that, otherwise I'll have to tell everyone what you got up to at Kate and Tom's wedding?

RORY: *(Gasps)* We were in a normal sauna and there was a normal swing and that's the end of the story.

KATE: Wait, what happened at our wedding?

TOM: No sex, that's what happened.

KATE: Oh, I'm sorry you didn't get your three minutes of fun.

TOM: Not tonight!

KATE: Fine! So…! Who else is joining us?

MICHAEL: I guess it's just us now that Max had to cancel.

KATE: Oh, I just saw the extra wine glasses and just thought?

MICHAEL: What? Wait, why is there eight glasses out? I only put out six.

JACOB: *(Getting nervous)* Is there?

MICHAEL: Did you put extra glasses out?

JACOB: *(Extremely nervous)* Did I?

MICHAEL: Why would you put two extra glasses out? Have you invited more people?

JACOB: *(Choking)* Have I?

MICHAEL: Who did you invite?

[Awkward silence.]

JACOB: Have I?

MICHAEL: Sweetie, I don't get what the big deal is, I don't mind if you've invited more people. In fact, the more the merrier I say! Unless of course you invited... No!

JACOB: *(Terrified)* Have I?

MICHAEL: Jacob!

JACOB: Look I can explain.

MICHAEL: Please don't tell me you invited... *Him*!

JACOB: I thought we agreed not to use masculine pronouns when talking about my sister?

MICHAEL: Consider it something else to put on the shelf!

JACOB: Ok, just hear me out... She called me last minute –

MICHAEL: **Ok, so the Hulk called you last minute-*

JACOB: Michael, stop!

MICHAEL: I just don't understand why you would invite her tonight, of all nights, when you know how much tonight means to me.

JACOB: Michael, you know I wouldn't do anything to ruin your special night.

RORY: What's so special about tonight?

MICHAEL: Take some poppers Rory!

TOM: *(To Rory)* Can I try them?

KATE: You are just never happy with what you've got!

TOM: Kate! You promised.

KATE: Oh, don't worry I'm not going to say anything.

TOM: Thank –

KATE: Tom wants us to have a threesome.

TOM: Kate!

JACOB: Oh, Kate I'm…

MICHAEL: Oh, no, no, no! Don't try to change the subject.

JACOB: It wasn't me that brought the threesome up.

KATE: Look Tom that's another relationship you have ruined.

TOM: I didn't do anything.

JACOB: Tom, its fine you never-

MICHAEL: Yeah, this is all Jacob's doing.

RORY: Why am I even here?

JACOB: This is not my fault.

[Doorbell rings.]

MICHAEL: Is that her already?

JACOB: Well, I…

MICHAEL: She is already he – when were you planning to – Jacob I could just – *(stops breathing)*

JACOB: Michael? What are you doing? Come on, Michael, we have been through this! Remember what the doctor said? You are better than this.

[Doorbell rings.]

[Michael stops breathing harder.]

JACOB: Michael breathe!

[Michael gasps for air.]

RORY: *(Holding the poppers)* I bet everyone would love some of these right about now.

JACOB: Yes ok, that's her but…

MICHAEL: I didn't know dogs could ring doorbells.

JACOB: Please listen, she already knew about… you know, the thing? But I swear I didn't invite her. I made the mistake of telling her the plan and she called me up this evening saying she was in the area with a friend and wanted to say hello. I promise.

MICHAEL: Fine! But hurry we wouldn't want to keep the elephant man waiting.

JACOB: Michael.

MICHAEL: It's on the shelf!

[Jacob exits. Silence.]

RORY: So, Tom you looking for another girl or boy? *(Winks.)*

[CLAIRE enters.]

CLAIRE: Oi, oi, everyone! The meat wagon has just arrived, let the party begin!

MICHAEL: *(Gritting his teeth)* Claire.

CLAIRE: Michael, oh aren't you brave for still wearing skinny jeans at your age.

RORY: She got you good.

MICHAEL: Have you changed your hair?

CLAIRE: No?

MICHAEL: Well, maybe you should.

RORY: Oh, and its one-all.

[Claire pinches Michael's back as they awkwardly hug.]

MICHAEL: Ouch!

CLAIRE: What?

MICHAEL: You just pinched – she just pinched me!

KATE: Michael, relax, her bracelets probably just got caught on your shirt.

CLAIRE: Yeah, Michael… relax.

MICHAEL: Fine… fine. So, Claire, where is your friend?

CLAIRE: He is just getting our bags from the car.

MICHAEL: Bags?

CLAIRE: Yeah, didn't Jacob tell you? We're crashing here for the night.

MICHAEL: *(Long inhale and exhale)* No, he didn't.

JACOB: *(Nervously)* I'm just gonna go put some fresh towels for you guys in the guest room, I'll just leave them *(to Michael) on the shelf.*

[Jacob leaves.]

MICHAEL: Ah, we'll be careful. Last time I checked that shelf was looking pretty full!

CLAIRE: So, were you planning on introducing me to your friends, or are you always this bad of a host?

KATE: Hi, I'm Kate, that is Michael's cousin Rory, and I think that's everyone who matters.

CLAIRE: Ok. I'm Claire, Jacob's sister.

MICHAEL: *(Coughing)* Basically brother.

[Claire stares at him.]

CLAIRE: And you are?

TOM: I'm tits – Tom – I'm Kate's husband.

KATE: You wouldn't know we are married because neither of us are happy.

CLAIRE: Ah, I was actually married once myself. Yeah, we lived on the beautiful sunny coast of... Essex and had our very own chinchilla farm. He didn't speak a word of English, but he knew body language. Every. Single. Word. His two favourite words you ask? Bus. Driver.

KATE: Bus driver?

CLAIRE: Yeah, it's when you are doing it doggy style and he puts his left thumb in your shitter moving it side to side like driving the bus? Then honks on your right titty like a horn. He was great.

KATE: What happened?

CLAIRE: He got deported.

KATE: Oh, I'm sorry to hear –

CLAIRE: Nah, it's ok - I was the one that reported him. So, you gay boy! *(To Rory)* What's your story? Tell me a bit about yourself.

RORY: Let's see, I hate my day job, I live with seven horrible strangers – three of whom are vegans – I'm alone, and I recently got a cat who pissed on my laptop then ran away.

CLAIRE: *(To Michael)* You have some interesting friends.

MICHAEL: Well, I'm sorry, like everything else they aren't up to your standards.

CLAIRE: Bitchy and passive aggressive, really living up to that gay stereotype, aren't you?

MICHAEL: *(Fake laughing and smiling through his teeth)* I fucking hate you.

CLAIRE: Now, now, Michael. I didn't come here to fight.

MICHAEL: No, you clearly came here to stink up my living room with that musky men's aftershave.

CLAIRE: That reminds me I'm actually selling perfumes for men and women at the minute, if anyone is interested?

KATE: **Oh, is that like from Avon?*

CLAIRE: No? It's from the boot of my car.

KATE: Oh ok, we're very different people.

[SHANE enters holding two bags.]

SHANE: Hey, sorry, umm, I'm Shane. I'm friends with Jacob and Claire.

MICHAEL: Oh, hi – *(Noticing his good looks)* Hi! I'm Michael, please, have a seat and you can just put those bags in the corner.

[Rory and Michael make crude gestures.]

CLAIRE: Guys, this is Shane. Jacob and I knew him from back home. So, this is Kate and her husband Tom, and this is- sorry I completely forgot your name.

RORY: Of course, you did!

MICHAEL: Ignore him, he's high on poppers. Can I get you a drink?

SHANE: Yes, please! White would be great.

[Michael pours Shane a glass.]

CLAIRE: I will take one of those too.

MICHAEL: Yeah, well you know where the bottle is. So, Shane, I didn't realise you also knew Jacob?

SHANE: Yeah, you could say we were very close a few years back – but I moved to the US. I've just moved home recently because my grandmother passed away and I wanted to be there for my family.

MICHAEL: Oh, I'm so sorry to hear.

RORY: Oh Shane, I know how it feels. I too am still getting over a loss.

SHANE: Oh, I'm sorry, who was it?

RORY: **Chariots in Vauxhall.*

SHANE: Ok.

[Michael passes Shane his glass of wine.]

SHANE: Thanks. So, how do you know Jacob?

MICHAEL: Oh, well I'm his partner.

SHANE: Oh.

[Jacob enters.]

JACOB: Ok, that's the room all set... Shane.

SHANE: Jacob...

JACOB: Shane...

SHANE: (*Glaring at Claire*) Jacob!

RORY: Its Rory, by the way. In case you cared.

JACOB: What are you doing here?

CLAIRE: Surprise! He moved back a few months ago and I just had to surprise you!

MICHAEL: Aww, look how shocked you are – that's so cute!

KATE: Yeah, Jacob you look like you've seen a ghost.

RORY: If all ghosts look this good, then as Haley Joel Osmond once said, I see dead people. *(Wiggles tongue)*

CLAIRE: These Brownies are kind of dry Michael.

MICHAEL: I'm sure that's just your skin.

CLAIRE: You should try my brownies recipe sometime, Michael. They don't contain any shellfish whatsoever.

[Michael Glares.]

MICHAEL: Ok, so does everyone have a drink?

TOM: Can I actually get some more?

KATE: *(Mutters in gibberish)*

CLAIRE: I'm loving this duo, you guys remind me of a partner I once had when I took a gap year to backpack, we argued like crazy.

KATE: I'd love to do that, where did you backpack?

CLAIRE: Oh, I went all over… Blackpool. You ever have a guy spit in your mouth on the Pepsi Max?

KATE: Aww, I'm uncomfortable talking to you.

CLAIRE: What's actually uncomfortable is the Blackpool tower.

KATE: Oh, we went up that –

CLAIRE: No! I mean when the guy lies flat on his back, and you spread your legs and drop down onto it.

KATE: I'd like this to be over.

RORY: **Do you guys remember the play I did in 'Above the Stag' where I played a backpacker?*

MICHAEL: Oh, yeah! What was that called again?

KATE: Homeward Pound?

RORY: Nope not that one.

JACOB: Good Will Humping!

RORY: Nope.

TOM: Mary Poppers.

RORY: Before that one.

MICHAEL: Cumty Dumpty.

RORY: After that one.

KATE: Fister Act 2.

JACOB: The Squirt Locker?

MICHAEL: The Fairy-Man.

TOM: Captain Americock.

JACOB: Bi-Tanic.

KATE: Mountain tops! And bottoms!

RORY: That's the one!

KATE: That was the best one!

TOM: The audience participation made it even more interesting.

RORY: **Ah, good times. Until they shut down without notice.*

SHANE: You seemed to have done a lot of shows in that one venue?

RORY: They like to use the same actors a lot.

MICHAEL: Ok, so Shane and It, we have these game nights every few months and we have a little bit of a tournament going on with me and Jacob way in the lead but because you guys are new, I think if everyone is ok, we can just start a fresh score board for tonight?

CLAIRE: Oh.

MICHAEL: Is something wrong?

CLAIRE: Oh no, I just thought this was a party. *(Laughs)*

MICHAEL: *(Looks at Jacob)* Wow.

JACOB: *(Mouths)* I love you.

MICHAEL: Ok, let's get into teams and we can start the games; we have uneven numbers but I'm sure it will be fine if we have one team of three.

KATE: Oh, I'm sure Tom will love that.

MICHAEL: Again, just ignoring that I think the fair thing to do is just put everyone's name in a cup and see who is teamed up. Is that fair? I have always been prepared for a situation like this.

[As Michael walks to the table Claire trips him and he falls.]

CLAIRE: Wow, bit too much to drink Michael?

JACOB: Are you ok?

MICHAEL: She tripped me!

CLAIRE: I would never!

JACOB: I… I didn't see I'm sorry.

[Michael goes to shout but Jacob rushes to him.]

Michael – Michael, don't let her get to you remember, this is your night it's all about you.

MICHAEL: Ok, ok.

[After writing everyone's names down and putting them into a cup.]

CLAIRE: *(Emotionless)* The anticipation is killing me.

RORY: *(To Michael)* She is burning you tonight.

[Michael mocks Claire.]

JACOB: Michael.

MICHAEL: No, you're right, I won't stoop to her childish and immature level.

CLAIRE: What was that?

MICHAEL: *(Childish screaming)* I didn't say anything!

[Michael composes himself.]

Ok, so the first team is Shane and Jacob – aww, it's a little chance for you guys to catch up! The second team is me and… oh who will it be? Drumroll, please.

[A very lacklustre drum roll from the party.]

It's… Claire. So, I guess that means you guys will be a three.

RORY: It's not the threesome you imagined, Tom, but it could be better than you ever dreamed.

MICHAEL: *(Aside to Jacob)* Ok, so even though there may not be a wedding as I'm planning on killing you, I think what we should do is do a few rounds of the game, then I will give you a signal when we can do the announcement.

JACOB: *(Aside to Michael)* Look before you do…

MICHAEL: Shane, we pulled your name out first, so why don't you start? Ok everybody let's get into our teams.

SHANE: Ah, ok.

RORY: Shane you are so funny! I'm not sure if Michael mentioned this, we play strip charades, so every time someone guesses it wrong something's gotta come off.

TOM: *(Aside to Kate)* Can you please stop with these digs, ok? I said I was sorry! I will take the threesome idea off the table.

KATE: *(Aside to Tom)* We are not having a threesome on a table!

TOM: *(Aside to Kate)* That's not what I sa – oh, forget it. You know what? Maybe I do want that threesome. *(To Claire)* You! Backpacker! Would you like a threesome?

[Tom exits.]

CLAIRE: Now it's a party. *(Aside to Kate)* If you don't mind me saying, threesomes are pretty fun! I had one with two guys once, you ever heard of a spit roast?

KATE: *(Aside to Claire)* No, I don't think...

CLAIRE: *(Aside to Kate)* Or this other time, I was lying on my chest on a swing – in a gay sauna actually - and it was just like Superman flying on repeat you know? Like the love song? (*raps*) Watch me crank dat soulja boy, now superman that hoe? Like if someone had the superman movie on rewind and then fast forward, rewind and then fast forward I'm talking the Henry Cavill one, cause have you seen him in that suit? I'd go down so fast on that dick he'd forget all about Lois Lane. Do you see what I'm trying to say Kate?

KATE: *(Aside to Claire)* That you're a nymphomaniac?

CLAIRE: *(Aside to Kate)* Yes! But also, threesomes are fun... fucking fun!

MICHAEL: *(Aside to Claire)* Ok, Claire before you verbally violate Kate anymore, I don't think the actual threesome is the problem; it's the trust that's broken within her marriage.

KATE: *(Aside to Michael)* It's also the idea of another woman being there – I'd be worried he liked her more than me.

CLAIRE: *(Aside to Kate)* I'm sure he would never do that! You are a sexy girl *(Awkward silence.)* You just need to have faith in your man, I mean look at Michael, he has full trust in Jacob and isn't even worried that Shane is his ex!

MICHAEL: *(Aside to Claire)* Yeah, I actually agree you just- WHAT?

RORY: She said Shane is Jacob's ex! Oh, and by the way yeah, we can all hear you.

[Silence.]

SHANE: Maybe I should just take off?

RORY: Maybe you should just take off your top? What who said that?

JACOB: Michael, can I talk to you for a second?

MICHAEL: No, it's fine- everything is fine… we all have ex's, let's continue with the game.

JACOB: Are you sure?

MICHAEL: Yes, it's fine. *(Nipping Jacob)* I'm going to make you bleed. Let's play the game!

**[Shane pulls out his first charade card. It is 'Ex on the beach.' He is very uncomfortable and hesitant. He sheepishly starts acting it out.*

When no one is guessing he eventually gives up and points to Jacob who quickly realises.]

JACOB: **Ex on the beach.*

TOM: *(Entering)* Sorry guys, I'm sure you have all been wondering where I've been. What have I missed?

RORY: *Well, Claire got 'supermanned' by two guys, you know when you sit on your stomach and go back and forth on a swing? (*Raps*) 'Watch me crank dat soulja boy, now superman that hoe.' You know, we've all done it. Then Shane had *'Ex on the beach'* and it's funny, 'cause he's Jacobs ex, and Michael just found out – *gasp*! – and I think Kate still hates you... because of the threesome thing... but you know about that. And that's what you missed on *GLEE!*

KATE: Ok, why don't I take my turn.

CLAIRE: *(Sexually)* Yeah, you get up there.

RORY: So, what are you? Straight? Lesbian?

CLAIRE: Oh, please, the only lesbian in here is Michael.

RORY: Burn!

CLAIRE: The way I see it everyone is on the spectrum. We only live once, so why restrict yourself to just one thing? Like, take this room for example, everyone in here is pretty much moving along the spectrum.

TOM: Well, not me. I'd say I'm right at the end of it.

RORY: Yeah, the rear end, homo.

KATE: Ok, this is an easy one, guys.

[She motions a one-word film: the answer is 'Scream,' however she motions a guy with a hook.]

TOM: *Hook*!

KATE: No.

[She continues.]

TOM: Sweetie, I really think its *Hook*.

KATE: It's not fucking hook, it's a horror!

MICHAEL: You can't speak.

JACOB: She was…

MICHAEL: I wouldn't advise you to speak, either.

TOM: What one-word horror film is about a hook?

KATE: You know this, Tom. We have watched it together!

RORY: Is it *Hook*?

TOM: I can only think of '*I know what you did last summer*'?!

KATE: No, Tom, why can't you remember?

MICHAEL: Shh!

TOM: Do something else!

KATE: Guess something else!

RORY: I know what it is!

TOM: What?

RORY: *Hook*.

KATE: Tom! It has that girl *Buffy* in it!

TOM: What girl?

KATE: You know *that* girl?

TOM: That doesn't help!

KATE: You know the one, she has blonde hair!

MICHAEL: You can't speak!

CLAIRE: You're really fun, Michael.

JACOB: Claire!

KATE: She was in that TV show!

TOM: Why are all your clues so vague?

KATE: It's so fucking easy, Tom!

CLAIRE: Times up!

KATE: *Scream*!

TOM: The killer doesn't use a hook!

KATE: Yes, he does!

TOM: No! That's the one where they call them asking what their favourite scary movie is!

KATE: No, you idiot! That's *Scary Movie*! *Scream* is the one where they run a guy over in the summer and throw his body in the ocean, then a year later he comes back for revenge leaving them a note saying he knows what they did –

TOM: Last summer!

RORY: I'm pretty sure it was *Hook*.

CLAIRE: Ok, let's just say you are both right and we can just give you the point.

MICHAEL: That's not how the game goes.

SHANE: Maybe we should play a different game?

MICHAEL: Oh, what would you like to play? Maybe with my man?

JACOB: Michael!

RORY: You can play with me.

CLAIRE: Ok, everyone, enough! Look, it's my turn – let's all just try to remember it's only a game.

[She begins to go through the possibilities realising they are all bad for the situation.]

CLAIRE: Nope, can't do that. Not that one – oh, *Snakes on a Plane*! That's a great movie! I've had a snake on a plane once if you know what I mean? Ay? Ironically, I was a snake charmer at the time.

JACOB: Claire?

CLAIRE: Sorry, nope- God not that- next- no- umm, ok this works! *(To Rory)* You will like this one. *(Nudges him)*

RORY: **Umm can you not touch me please? Hashtag me too.*

KATE: **Rory! You can't joke about that!*

RORY: **Oh, it's ok – I'm gay.*

KATE: **What does that mean?*

RORY: **I don't know, but if it's a good enough excuse for Kevin Spacey it's good enough for me.*

KATE: **Rory!*

TOM: Kate, leave him alone, It's not that big of a deal.

KATE: Oh, well, speaking of things that aren't that big…

[Kate gestures down at Tom's crotch]

Tom?

[Tom gestures at Kates boobs]

TOM: Kate?

CLAIRE: Anyway.

[She acts out cat in the hat.]

MICHAEL: Cat in the hat!

CLAIRE: Yes!

RORY: I cannot believe you would bring up cats when you know my cat just pissed on my laptop and ran away! I should just storm out right now!

[Rory gets more comfortable and has more wine.]

RORY: Well, I'm not going to; this night is just getting good.

SHANE: *(To Jacob)* Do you remember the day we saw that film in the cinema?

JACOB: *(Clearly embarrassed)* Oh, God, I forgot about that.

SHANE: Remember that ushers face when he caught us?

JACOB: He didn't know where to look!

SHANE: I bet they still have our pictures up on the wall of shame!

JACOB: I forgot about the wall of shame!

SHANE: And in the picture your hair was clearly covered in...

[Michael stands up.]

MICHAEL: You know what? Maybe we should just take a break from charades- Oh, look! We seem to be almost out of white wine. Jacob why don't you help me get another bottle from the kitchen?

JACOB: *(Nervous)* Umm, I think I will just stay here.

MICHAEL: No, no. I think I really need your help.

JACOB: But there is almost a full bottle of white right here.

[Michael attempts to sink the whole bottle - it mostly pours all over him.]

MICHAEL: Nope, empty too.

[They both leave.]

RORY: I'm so sorry for your loss.

CLAIRE: My loss?

RORY: Yeah, your brother? 'Cause he's a dead man.

SHANE: *(To Claire)* Claire, I can't believe you didn't tell me he was with someone?

CLAIRE: They aren't even that serious, trust me I know he still has feelings for you.

KATE: Umm, they have been together for six years.

RORY: The first year doesn't count.

SHANE: Six years? Claire!

CLAIRE: Oh, that's nothing! I've had STI's longer than that.

SHANE: Claire, I can't believe you wouldn't – really?

KATE: Yeah, really?

RORY: I'm like the worst representation of the slutty gay stereotype and even I think that's bad.

CLAIRE: **Hey! Do you know how hard it is to get an appointment in Dean Street these days?*

KATE: She's right.

TOM: She is.

RORY: I've had a rash for a while now, and I should be *very* worried about it.

SHANE: Look that doesn't matter, what matters is that I didn't come here to separate a relationship!

RORY: How about separating my legs?

CLAIRE: You have no shame, do you…? I like you.

SHANE: Claire, we need to go.

CLAIRE: No, we should stay.

SHANE: Come on, Claire! This is serious, ok? We aren't teenagers anymore! You know what us breaking up did to me. It took me years to get over Jacob so when you told me he still had feelings for me all that stuff came rushing back! I came here thinking I had a chance with him. Rory, back me up here – if you were in my shoes, wouldn't you want to leave? I mean how awkward would you feel knowing the love of your life was settled down with someone when you came back to see them hoping to get close again?

[Pause.]

RORY: I have zero gag reflex.

[They all stare at Rory.]

SHANE: Claire, we need to go.

CLAIRE: No, I need you here.

SHANE: Why?

CLAIRE: Because you are the only one that can stop their engagement!

KATE: What?

MICHAEL: *[Offstage.]* This is all your fault!

[Slap.]

JACOB: *[Offstage.]* Ouch!

[Both enter, Michael carrying wine.]

MICHAEL: We have wine! [Awkward pause.] What?

KATE: You guys are engaged?

MICHAEL: No! *(Trying to laugh it off)* Who wants wine?

KATE: Yes, you are.

MICHAEL: *(Pouring Rory more wine while trying to smile.)* No, you must have me mistaken with someone else.

[Now spilling wine.]

KATE: That's an engagement ring.

MICHAEL: No, it's not!

KATE: Michael, yes, it is.

MICHAEL: No, it's not, you nosey bitch!

KATE: Michael!

MICHAEL: Fine! How the hell did you find out?

CLAIRE: Erm, I think they just noticed the ring.

RORY: Claire told us. What?! I never said I liked you.

JACOB: Claire, you promised!

CLAIRE: It slipped out!

RORY: *(To Shane)* Nothing slips out of me. (Whispers, seductively.) Nothing!

MICHAEL: This is unbelievable. All I wanted was to just have a cute little celebration, but you just had to show up and ruin everything as usual. Well, you know what? No, I'm not going to let you ruin this for us. Screw it! Yes, we're engaged!

KATE: Oh, congratulations!

RORY: Ooh, you come here to me!

MICHAEL: Kate, Rory, I would love it if you could both be a part of the wedding.

KATE: I'd love to!

RORY: Oh, I already know how I will start my best man speech. This one time, on a swing in the gay sauna…

MICHAEL: Stop!

KATE: I wish we had some champagne to celebrate.

MICHAEL: We have some iced in the kitchen.

TOM: If you said in advance, we could have just chilled them on my blue balls.

KATE: Or against your mother's heart.

TOM: Leave my mother out of this.

KATE: Fuck your mother!

[Kate storms out.]

JACOB: Michael, I'm really sorry about –

MICHAEL: You know what? It's ok, I know you didn't mean for any of this to happen.

JACOB: And Claire? Do you have something to say to Michael?

CLAIRE: Congratulations?

JACOB: Claire.

CLAIRE: Fine! I'm sorry I crashed your little party.

[Kate enters.]

KATE: Michael, I can't find the glasses. Just Like Tom can't find the G-spot.

MICHAEL: It's ok I'll get them. *(To Claire)* Shove your apology up your fat arse.

[Claire pushes Michael who falls flat on the ground.]

MICHAEL: Ok, did anyone see her do that?

ALL: No.

MICHAEL: Seriously?

[Michael exits.]

TOM: Jacob, I'm sorry we have been so immature tonight.

KATE: Yeah, I'm so sorry for Tom's behaviour.

TOM: *(Very drunk looking at no one)* You shut up!

JACOB: It's fine

TOM: Apology accepted.

JACOB: I'm more annoyed at my evil sister here! What were you thinking inviting him? No offence, Shane, it's really nice to see you but you really shouldn't have come here.

SHANE: Jacob, I honestly didn't know you were even seeing anyone. Claire here, made it sound like you were recently single so I thought it would be nice to catch up that's all. I swear I didn't know you were engaged again.

RORY: It's my birthday by the way.

JACOB: Why would you make him think that? You knew about tonight and know how much I love Michael. Claire, Shane means nothing to me – it was a stupid childish fling when I was young and immature; us breaking up was the best thing that ever happened to me.

SHANE: *(Upset)* Hey!

RORY: Thought this was gonna be a surprise party.

JACOB: I didn't even know what love was at that age. It was such a silly relationship that I never even thought it was worth telling Michael about. Shane is nothing compared to Michael.

SHANE: *(Visibly angry)* Excuse me?

RORY: Not even a balloon.

CLAIRE: Jacob, just hear me out, ok? Say what you want but I've never seen you so happy than when you were with Shane.

JACOB: What is your problem with Michael? He has tried so hard for you to like him.

CLAIRE: Oh, don't try to defend him! You know what he is like to me.

RORY: Wait did he say engaged… again?

[Silence.]

JACOB: No.

KATE: Yes, he did? Oh, my god when you said they were exes, did you mean ex-fiancé?

RORY: You guys suck at keeping secrets. *(To Shane)* I suck too. *Fuck*!

JACOB: Look, Michael doesn't know and you can't tell him. You guys seen how upset he got before. Please, please don't make tonight any worse for him.

RORY: I love it, you know just when you think everyone has made up and it's all peaceful then *bam*! We are back in it again. Round two. I love it!

KATE: I'm sorry but you can't expect me to keep a secret like this from my best friend.

JACOB: You won't have to get us a wedding gift.

KATE: Ok then, continue.

TOM: Kate, are you serious? That's your best friend.

KATE: Oh, don't you start on loyalty.

TOM: Kate, I didn't…

KATE: Didn't what? Didn't mean it? Oh, please don't think I don't see you interviewing every girl we pass with your eyes to see if she would work for this threesome you have in mind.

TOM: When have I ever done that?

KATE: Well, from the moment Claire walked in, you haven't taken your eyes off her tits. I mean yes, they are big but like –

[Kate rips her top open.]

Are these not big enough for you? Huh? Are these not big enough?

RORY: *(In disbelief of what he just saw.)* How strong are these poppers?

[Michael enters with a tray with glasses of champagne.]

MICHAEL: Ok, everybody… what the hell have I missed?

JACOB: Nothing, everything is fine! Let's all gather round for a toast then, eh?

[Jacob passes everyone a glass of champagne and they hold their glasses up to toast.]

To Michael, the only person I have ever - or will ever – love.

SHANE: Fuck you, Jacob!

[Shane throws his drink over Jacob.]

MICHAEL: Hey!

[Michael throws his drink over Shane.]

CLAIRE: Leave him alone!

[Throws her drink over Michael.]

JACOB: Claire!

[Throws his drink over Claire.]

KATE: Stop looking at her wet tits!

[Throws her drink over Tom.]

TOM: I wasn't!

[Throws his drink over Kate. Pause. Rory pours his drink over himself.]

RORY: That's fine guys I'll just do it myself!

[Blackout.]

ACT 2

Italicized dialogue beginning with '' is open for modification to modern pop culture and current affairs.*

[All characters begin backstage overlapping lines until they are centre stage reaching a crescendo]

MICHAEL: I'm engaged!

JACOB: He is going to kill me.

KATE: I hope your dick falls off!

TOM: I hope your cunt dries up!

RORY: What the hell?

CLAIRE: Oi Oi everyone.

SHANE: Maybe I should take off.

MICHAEL: Let's play the game!

JACOB: The wall of shame!

KATE: Fuck your mother!

TOM: Cancer killed my dad.

RORY: It's my birthday!

CLAIRE: Bus. Driver.

SHANE: Excuse me!

MICHAEL: It's on the shelf!

JACOB: Look I can explain!

KATE: Tom wants to have a threesome.

TOM: Blue balls!

RORY: Zero Gag reflex.

CLAIRE: Now it's a party.

SHANE: We need to leave.

MICHAEL: Nosey bitch!

JACOB: I love you.

KATE: Scream!

TOM: Backpacker.

RORY: **Chariots.*

CLAIRE: Pepsi Max.

SHANE: Claire!

MICHAEL: Rory!

JACOB: Michael!

KATE: Tom!

TOM: Tits!

RORY: Cat!

CLAIRE: Shane!

SHANE: Fuck you, Jacob!

[Shane throws his drink over Jacob.]

MICHAEL: Hey!

[Michael throws his drink over Shane.]

CLAIRE: Leave him alone!

[Throws her drink over Michael.]

JACOB: Claire!

[Throws his drink over Claire.]

KATE: Stop looking at her wet tits!

[Throws her drink over Tom.]

TOM: I wasn't!

[Throws his drink over Kate. Pause. Rory pours his drink over himself.]

RORY: That's fine guys I'll just do it myself!

[Silence.]

MICHAEL: What the hell was that all about?

KATE: He just keeps looking at women's tits and...

MICHAEL: Will you shut up about tits I was talking to Shane and Jacob!

SHANE: It doesn't matter! Look, Michael, I'm really sorry for getting in the way of your big night, but I think I should go.

MICHAEL: *(Mocking Shane)* Oh, I think I should go! *Really?* You think?

RORY: *(Trying to stop him from leaving)* No, Shane, I think you should stay because... *(Rubs his chest)* because... because... what was I going to say?

SHANE: No, I really should go.

RORY: Why don't you at least let your top dry off before you go out into the cold? Brrr.

SHANE: It's not even that bad.

[Rory takes the flower vase from the table and throws the water over Shane's top.]

RORY: Oh, look at me and my butter fingers! Why don't you take that off and I will grab you one of Michael's tops?

MICHAEL: Are you kidding me?

SHANE: Fine, I will stay but just until it at least stops snowing outside.

[Shane takes his top off revealing his perfect body and chiselled abs.]

RORY: Jesus Christ! Let me show you to the bathroom- Oh, hold on, I forgot my poppers.

SHANE: Why do you need poppers to show me to the bathroom?

RORY: You ask a lot of questions, don't you, Shane! Now, you guys sit down, relax, and don't do anymore fighting until I get back! This is all I have.

[Rory leaves with Shane to get a top and the rest of the group awkwardly sit down. Long silence. Claire provocatively starts drying the floor with a throw from her chair, staring at Tom and Kate the entire time.]

CLAIRE: I'm sorry about my tits, Kate.

KATE: I guess it's not really your fault, they are very pretty.

CLAIRE: I tell yah, if I had a pound for every time these bad boys ruined a marriage... I'd have fourteen pounds by the way... fourteen!

MICHAEL: So, how long did you and Shane go out for? Was he better than me? Don't answer that! Was he? Don't! Did you bottom for him?

JACOB: Who cares, Michael? We all have pasts, ok? I've had boyfriends and you've had swings in saunas.

MICHAEL: Are you serious?

CLAIRE: That was a bad idea, Jacob.

KATE: Terrible.

TOM: Unforgivable.

MICHAEL: Are you really slut shaming me right now?

KATE: **It's twenty-twenty-three, Jacob! We don't slut shame anymore.*

TOM: You just shamed me for wanting a threesome.

KATE: You're not a slut, you're a pig. Oink, oink, bitch!

CLAIRE: I eat bacon for breakfast.

KATE: We all eat bacon, calm down Chewbacca.

CLAIRE: Oh, I'll give you something to chew on.

[Claire rubs her nipple]

JACOB: No, no! Look, that's not what I meant, I just meant we all have a past, but it doesn't matter.

MICHAEL: Ok, well, if it doesn't matter, then you won't mind telling me how long you were together.

JACOB: But why does it matter so much?

CLAIRE: Five years.

JACOB: Claire! Look, yes, it sounds like a long time, and no, I didn't tell you... but I was just a young teenager, I didn't know any better. I should have told you, but when you think about it, the fact that it never crossed my mind proves how little I think of him; I basically forgot he existed, ok? It is fine, as you said: we all have exes.

MICHAEL: Yes, but none of ours are getting naked and probably touched up by Rory in our bathroom. Also, I'm sorry, but *look at him.*

JACOB: What about him?

MICHAEL: Well, I don't know, he just walked in here being all macho with his rugged face, being all tall with his tallness, with those big muscular arms, *(starting to get lost in thought)* and that… thick chest below that sharp jaw, and those eyes that could stare deep into your soul. And that ass!

KATE: Mmm! That ass!

MICHAEL: I mean even Tom was staring at him.

KATE: *(To tom)* You would think I'd be mad, but I wanna slap that ass and have it slap me right back.

MICHAEL: **I mean Jesus Christ, Jacob, you went from dating Zac Efron to Sue Perkins! Has he always looked like that?*

CLAIRE: He's actually lost some muscle

KATE: He can lose a muscle in me.

MICHAEL: And does he have any class? In the Cinema really? Covering your hair in God only knows what!

JACOB: First of all, my hair was covered in popcorn because we were having a food fight in the aisles. And so, what? Because he's a handsome guy you feel threatened? Michael how shallow do you think I am? Yes, I haven't seen him in a long time and yes in that time he has grown into a beautiful- ok person, but I don't care about any of that.

CLAIRE: Well duh, I mean you chose to be with this one…

RORY: *(Offstage)* She got you again!

JACOB: Michael? Michael, I love you, not Shane. Ok? I'm marrying you! Michael John Liam Casey, the most tightly wound, obsessive-compulsive, competitive, passionate, loving, and caring person I've ever met.

[Michael smirks.]

Michael, I want to be with you. I want to win charades with you. I want to watch Cat in the Hat with you. I really want to play on a swing with you. Ok?

MICHAEL: You're right. I'm sorry- it's just- I think this whole night has just made me a little crazy. I'm also very drunk from that bottle of wine.

[Jacobs laughs and kisses Michael.]

TOM: See, why can't we maturely work through our problems like that?

KATE: That is completely different! Michael is upset because Jacob's ex-fiancé is at their engagement party, whereas I'm upset because you want to have an open relationship.

MICHAEL: What did you say?

KATE: Dammit, Rory was right! We do suck at that!

MICHAEL: You were engaged?

JACOB: *(To Kate)* You owe us a wedding gift!

KATE: No, no! What I meant to say was: ex-boyfriend. They weren't engaged.

CLAIRE: Yes, they were.

KATE: You are not a nice person.

JACOB: *(Trying to joke)* How about we put it on the shelf?

MICHAEL: Oh, ok let's try that… Umm, oh, look, the shelf fell down!

[Michael goes to storm out.]

CLAIRE: If it makes you feel any better, I will admit you suit our grandmothers ring much better than Shane did.

KATE: Well, there really is no saving that one.

MICHAEL: I actually don't know what to say.

CLAIRE: That's a first.

KATE: Leave him alone!

TOM: Kate, stay out of it!

JACOB: Yeah, for once keep your nose out of other people's problems.

MICHAEL: Leave her alone!

CLAIRE: Oh, shut up, Michael and stop bossing him around.

KATE: What is your problem?

TOM: Katherine!

[They all begin to shout over each other frantically as Rory enters carrying the board game 'Twister'.]

RORY: Who wants to play *Twister*?

[They don't even notice he is there as they continue to argue. Rory slams the board game to the floor loudly.]

RORY: Who wants to play twister!

[They all jump at his screaming and stop.]

RORY: Yay, Twister.

KATE: Sorry, Rory, but I think Tom and I need to leave.

TOM: Actually, I love twister.

CLAIRE: *(Getting very close to Tom)* So do I.

KATE: Let's do this!

MICHAEL: Wait, look I think its best if everyone goes home. Clearly, me and Jacob have a few things to talk about, and I just wanna say I'm really sorry about tonight, ok? It's all my fault.

JACOB: No, it's not.

MICHAEL: Well, of course it's not my fault, I was just being polite! This is all you and this wannabe amateur porn star's fault.

[Michael storms out.]

SHANE: Jacob, are you still as flexible as you used to be?

[Michael storms in.]

MICHAEL: Let's play the fucking game!

JACOB: Michael, shouldn't we –

MICHAEL: Rory! Grab the table!

KATE: Yeah, grab it bitch!

JACOB: Michael, just wait –

KATE: *(To Tom)* Yeah, just you wait bitch!

RORY: *(Pushing the table to the side and putting the mat down)* I've got a semi I'm that excited!

KATE: So. Do. I. Bitch! *(Tugs on her imaginary balls)*

CLAIRE: How about we make this more interesting, then?

KATE: What did you have in mind?

CLAIRE: Ok, Kate, if you are the last standing, Tom drops this threesome thing forever, but if he wins you have to have the threesome with a girl of his choice.

KATE: And what if you win?

CLAIRE: I get to choose the girl. *(Rubs against Tom)*

JACOB: Kate, maybe you should –

KATE: Deal!

JACOB: Continue to ignore me.

CLAIRE: Michael? Wanna get involved?

MICHAEL: What could you possibly offer me?

CLAIRE: If you win, I will leave and not come to your wedding.

MICHAEL: Ok…

CLAIRE: But! If Shane wins? You have to end the engagement.

[Silence.]

RORY: Ok, now I am fully erect.

KATE: *(Whispers)* Me too, bitch.

MICHAEL: Deal!

JACOB: Michael!

MICHAEL: It's fine, I've got this.

JACOB: Shane, if you actually care about me, you won't be a part of this.

SHANE: Nah, I think I'm gonna play. After all, why would I care about you or your partner? I'm just a childish fling and wannabe porn star.

MICHAEL: Don't worry, Jacob, I've always been good at *Twister.*

CLAIRE: Yeah, I'm sure you will be fine. Oh, by the way, Shane, what is it you do for a living?

SHANE: I'm a professional acrobatic gymnast.

[Silence. Rory starts clapping.]

MICHAEL: Just spin the thingy!

JACOB: Ok, fine, but if I win everyone has to stop all this childish arguing and go home!

RORY: Ok, I'm going to choose people at random so everyone get ready.

KATE: Yeah, get ready to lose, bitch!

[They begin to play Twister getting into increasingly sexual positions.]

RORY: The time has come for you to Twister... For. Your. Lives-ives-ives! Good luck, and don't fuck it up.

[Rory stands up on the sofa looking down on all of them.]

RORY: Ok, first up: Tom, right foot, red. *(Fourth circle across)*

Next: Kate, left hand, green *(Sixth circle across)*

KATE: I'm basically winning!

RORY: Ok, Jacob, left foot yellow. *(First circle across)*

Ah, Michael, left leg, blue. *(Sixth circle across)*

Claire, right foot, blue. *(Fourth circle across)*

And that leaves: Shane, right hand, green. *(First circle across. Grazes Jacobs leg.)*

Back to Tom, left foot, red. *(Third circle across)*

Kate, left foot, green. *(Fifth circle across)*

Who was next? Ahh, Jacob, right foot, yellow. *(Second circle across.)*

Ok, Michael, left leg, blue. *(Sixth circle across)*

Claire, left leg, blue. *(Third circle across)*

And, Shane, left hand, green. *(Second circle across)*

SHANE: Oh, Déjà vu.

MICHAEL: Rory!

RORY: Don't blame me, it's the fate of the spinner. So, moving on! Tom, right foot, red. *(Fifth circle across)*

Kate, right hand *green (Fourth circle across)*

KATE: Yes! Nailed it!

RORY: Ok, sweetie, no more of that.

Jacob, right hand, green. *(Third circle across)*

Michael, left leg, blue. *(Sixth circle across)*

MICHAEL: Seriously?

RORY: Ok, so the board is sensing you are very angry with it right now and thinks you need to just calm down.

Claire, right hand, yellow. *(Fourth circle across)*

CLAIRE: The last time I was in this position, I was kayaking through Benidorm.

KATE: Your stories suck!

CLAIRE: Suck better than you, from what I've heard.

RORY: Shane, left hand, yellow. *(Third circle across)*

SHANE: You still make that face when you get nervous, I always loved that.

MICHAEL: Yeah, well love fades! And so do freakishly good looks!

RORY: Umm, Michael, your negativity and terrible comebacks are really making me lose my erection, and I think that's just selfish so can we continue? Ok, good.

Tom, right hand, yellow. *(Fifth circle across)*

CLAIRE: Oh, Tom is that a bread roll in your pocket, or are you just happy to see me? *(Whispers)* I hope it's both.

RORY: Kate, right foot, red. *(Sixth circle across)*

KATE: Ok, let's see how I can do this. *(She falls)* No!

CLAIRE: Too bad, bitch!

RORY: Silence! And, Kate, that was an embarrassment; you really are a disgrace to all white woman everywhere.

Jacob, right hand, red. *(Second circle across)*

Michael, left leg, blue *(Sixth circle across)*

MICHAEL: Oh, come on!

RORY: Claire, right, freakishly small hand, green. *(Fourth circle across)*

And, Shane, right hand, red. *(First circle across)*

Ok, that one wasn't even me, it was just fate.

KATE: This is a stupid game!

RORY: You're a stupid game! Interrupt me again, and I swear to God, bitch! I swear to God! Now, Tom, right hand, green. *(Third circle across)*

[Tom falls onto Claire in a very sexual doggy style manner, both of them heavily grunting as they fall.]

TOM: No, wait don't move. Don't fucking move. Ah!

[Tom climbs off her.]

I'm so sorry.

CLAIRE: For what? I still came out of it a winner. *(To Kate)* Think I might be pregnant! What, what!

RORY: Jacob, left leg, yellow. *(Fourth circle across)*

Michael, left leg, blue. *(Sixth circle across)*

MICHAEL: Fuck you!

RORY: Shane, left leg, green. *(Fifth circle across)*

SHANE: You used to love sideways doggy.

MICHAEL: Hah, he still does! I don't know how that helped the situation.

RORY: Shane well played. Ok, let's keep going. Jacob, left leg, red. *(First circle across)* Michael...

MICHAEL: I dare you to say it.

RORY: Fine! Right leg, blue. *(Third circle across)*

MICHAEL: Gladly!

[Michael kicks Shane who then falls knocking Jacob over ending the game.]

SHANE: What the hell?

MICHAEL: Sorry, I slipped.

SHANE: Bullshit, that was on purpose!

KATE: Wait! If they fell, and Michael is disqualified, who is the winner?

RORY: We are all in our late twenties playing Twister on a Friday night, I don't think any of us are winners.

SHANE: I can't believe you kicked me because you can't handle your boyfriend has a past.

MICHAEL: Speaking of the past, go back there!

SHANE: Oh, what's wrong? Worried I might steal him back? Worried he loved me more?

MICHAEL: Clearly wasn't love if he forgot you that quickly.

SHANE: Forgetting something and keeping it a secret are two very different things.

MICHAEL: Yeh, your right. And your relationship was nothing but a dirty little secret that he was ashamed to tell me about. What does that say about you?

JACOB: Guys let's just…

SHANE: Oh please, the person he should be ashamed of is you. Typical fem gay man, always needing to be the centre of attention. Look at this night, it has nothing to do with your love for Jacob, it's all about you.

JACOB: Enough Shane.

MICHAEL: You want to talk about the typical gay man? Look at you. None of us could tell you anything about yourself because your entire personality is 'going to the gym'. I mean heaven forbid if someone didn't find you attractive because you'd have nothing to offer them. I may not be the picture-perfect person, but I love that man, I know him inside and out and he accepts me for more than just face value.

SHANE: *No, you know the Jacob you've molded. The one you've casted to play the perfect husband in 'Michael's perfect story'. I know the real Jacob. The one who says his favourite film is Shawshank so he can seem mature but really, it's *Toy Story*. The one who hated playing football but did it just to make his mum proud. The one who was devastated when his dad left. And I was the one to pick up the pieces, the one who cried with him, the one who made him laugh, the one that helped him move on. I know the real raw Jacob.

RORY: Say raw again.

MICHAEL: *First of all, it's *Toy Story 2, he loves himself a bit of Jessie.* And secondly, don't think for a single second that you know him better than I do. You might have helped make him a man, but I made him good at it.

SHANE: I know him better.

MICHAEL: I know him better!

SHANE: Favourite animal?

MICHAEL: Golden retriever. Favourite colour?

SHANE: Blue. Favourite season?

MICHAEL: Autumn. Mother's maiden name?

SHANE: Roberts. Favourite –

JACOB: Guys stop this is ridiculous.

CLAIRE: Jacob's right. This is ridiculous.

[Claire pulls out white boards from her bags in the corner].

We should make this a game so there is a clear winner.

RORY: Oh my god my semi's back!

KATE: So is mine, bitch.

MICHAEL: Wait did you bring these with you?

CLAIRE: Whatever, look do you want to play or not?

MICHAEL: No, I can't believe you planned this, you sick fuck.

[Michael storms out].

SHANE: He probably knows I will win.

[Michael storms in].

MICHAEL: Let's play the fucking game!

JACOB: Michael, will you stop doing that!

[Rory dramatically stands up. Everyone turns to him].

RORY: Once again, I am fully erect!

[Kate dramatically stands up. Everyone turns to her].

KATE: Me. Too. Bitch!

JACOB: Enough! Jesus, we are just going around in circles. What is wrong with you people? We are not playing a game to see which of my past and present fiancés know me better.

RORY: Boo!

MICHAEL: Jacob, look sweetie, I know tonight has been crazy and its nothing like we imagined it would be, but look at me, Jacob, I need you… to verify the answers so I can win your love.

JACOB: No!

[Jacob turns to leave but is met with Rory who grabs his top by the throat and pulls him into his face]

RORY: Listen to me you little prick. Now I have had a very shit night, ok? I've been locked outside, I've had to endure your horrible sister, I've lost my cat, and I've been ignored by the love of my life. This might be the only entertaining thing to come from this evening so you are gonna sit here and play the game so he can win your love, and I can be Shane's rebound, ok? And if you say no, so help me God, I'm gonna walk up those stairs, into your bedroom and I'm just gonna start pissing Jacob, just all over it.

[Kate leans in from nowhere].

KATE: And I'll piss in your Kettle.

JACOB: *(Terrified)* Ok, ok, we can play the game.

RORY: Good. I'm very sorry you all had to see that. Unless you like someone mean and aggressive like that Shane?

SHANE: Actually, I prefer someone sweet and innocent.

RORY: Good thing I'm a virgin then. Hymen.

CLAIRE: Ok let's do this, 5 Questions, Mr & Mrs Style, Winner wins Jacobs Love.

JACOB: No, the winner…

MICHAEL / SHANE: Deal!

JACOB: Can no one hear me?

TOM: I can

KATE: Who invited you?

CLAIRE: Ok! Question 1, What is Jacobs favourite drink?

[Jacob, Michael, and Shane write their answers on their boards]

Shane?

SHANE: G+T.

CLAIRE: Michael?

MICHAEL: Whiskey, 1 cubes of ice and a dash of water.

CLAIRE: Jacob?

JACOB: Whiskey, 1 cubes, dash of water.

MICHAEL: Eat my entire ass.

[Rory goes to whisper to Shane]

Rory!

[Rory sits down]

CLAIRE: Round one to Michaela. Next question. What is Jacob's biggest fear?

[Jacob, Michael, and Shane write their answers on their boards]

Michael?

MICHAEL: Losing a loved one.

CLAIRE: Shane?

SHANE: Losing his mum.

CLAIRE: Oooh, we have specifics, and the correct answer Jacob?

JACOB: My mum dying.

SHANE: Ha!

MICHAEL: Jacob what are you doing? We had a plan!

JACOB: No, we didn't?

MICHAEL: Ok, you're being hysterical.

CLAIRE: Michael, enough, that's one point to Shane. Although, Jacob, is your fear only for mum dying?

JACOB: Well…

KATE: Can we nominate a mother to die?

TOM: **Oh, shut up Ginny Weasley.*

KATE: Oh, I'm surprised you've paid enough attention to me to even notice I have ginger hair.

TOM: I pay lots of attention to you!

KATE: Oh please! I bet you couldn't answer any of these questions about me.

TOM: I know everything about you!

KATE: Oh yeh?

[Kate grabs two whiteboards from Claire's bag]

Let's do this then!

TOM: Winner wins Jacob's love!

JACOB: What?

KATE: Deal!

RORY: Guess I'll just watch alone then.

TOM: Don't worry Jacob, I won't lose this, you are my best friend.

JACOB: Tell me one thing you know about me.

[Silence]

TOM: Your favourite drink is losing your mother.

JACOB: Ok.

CLAIRE: Ok question 3. What is Jacob or Kate's best childhood memory?

[Everyone writes their answers]

Show your submitted answers.

SHANE: The day he got his pet dog Bella.

MICHAEL: First family holiday to the beach.

JACOB: Getting Bella.

SHANE: And I was there that day!

MICHAEL: Why do you hate me?

CLAIRE: Tom, what have you put for Kate's favourite childhood memory?

[Tom doesn't show his board]

TOM: When her adult fangs came through and she became a fully-fledged soul sucking vampire.

KATE: Like I'd ever suck you. The correct answer was when my Pony Lucinda won best in show.

RORY: You had a horse named Lucinda? Jesus you're hard to like.

CLAIRE: OK that's 2-1 to Shane and Tom zero. Question number 4. What was the name of Jacob's or Kate's first ever friend?

[Everyone writes their answers]

Answers?

SHANE: Easy, me.

MICHAEL: Actually, his first friend was Bob the Bob cat! He was Jacob's imaginary friend!

JACOB: Michael's Right.

CLAIRE: Even I knew about Bob, Shane.

MICHAEL: How does it feel, even an imaginary cat had a better personality than you?

CLAIRE: Tom, what did you write?

TOM: Oh, I just wrote her other personality since she is so two faced.

KATE: I'd rather have two faces than two chins.

TOM: You said you liked my chins!

KATE: And you said 'til death do us part' but here you are with your wandering eyes.

CLAIRE: **I dated someone with a wandering eye once, I met her back when I was the opening act for Liberty X.*

MICHAEL: Let me guess, you have some crude story about scissoring?

CLAIRE: Women don't actually Scissor Michael. We hole punch.

[She winks at Kate who grimaces]

RORY: I have a ho…

EVERYONE: Rory!

CLAIRE: Ok here it is… The final question… and we are neck to neck… Tom and Kate, you guys have to sit this one out. Its sudden death… Jacob… are you ready? Michael and Shane, the question is… coming now… here we go…

ALL: COME ON!

CLAIRE: Ok. Who does Jacob think is better in bed?

[Michael and Shane start writing]

JACOB: No, no, stop. That's enough.

MICHAEL: But I've almost won!

SHANE: Oh please, we all know I'm amazing in bed.

RORY: I hope you are, But Michael is the original Samantha of our group.

MICHAEL: Thank you, Rory.

KATE: Yeh but I bet Shane could fold it half and BP you by himself.

MICHAEL, RORY, SHANE, JACOB: DP.

JACOB: Look, that's not the point, ok? Let's stop this. I'm not answering a question like that.

CLAIRE: I agree, that wasn't a fair question.

JACOB: Thank you, ok so now that this is over…

CLAIRE: Ok new question!

JACOB: No!

EVERYONE ELSE: Yes!

CLAIRE: Final question, what is Jacobs favourite song?

MICHAEL: Easy.

SHANE: Too easy.

[Both write their answers]

CLAIRE: Answers?

[Both turn over their boards]

MICHAEL / SHANE: I don't want to miss a thing, Aerosmith.

CLAIRE: Jacob?

[Jacob reveals the same answer]

KATE: Oh my god it's a tie!

MICHAEL: I wrote it first!

SHANE: I wrote it first!

MICHAEL: It's our song!

SHANE: I used to sing it to him.

CLAIRE: Shane does have a beautiful singing voice.

SHANE: Do you remember Jacob?

JACOB: Oh, I don't… I think…

KATE: Sing it!

SHANE: What?

CLAIRE: Yeh Shane, sing it!

SHANE: Oh, I'm not…

[Rory pushes Jacob to the floor.]

RORY: Jesus Mary and Sarah Michelle Gellar sing the song.

SHANE: Ok, fine.

'I could stay awake just to hear you breathing,
Watch you smile while you are sleeping,
While you're far away and dreaming,
I could spend my life in this sweet surrender,
I could stay lost in the moment forever,

Cause every moment spent with you is a moment I treasure, forever and ever.'

[Shane gets very close to Jacob growing more sexual. Michael has grown very jealous at this so starts to sing badly trying to also be sexual]

MICHAEL / SHANE:

'I don't want to close my eyes,
I don't want to fall asleep,
Cause I'd miss you baby,
And I don't want to miss a thing,
Cause even when I dream of you
The sweetest dream will never do.
I don't want to miss one smile
And I don't want to miss one kiss
And I just want to be with you
Right here with you, just like this
And I just want to hold you close
I feel your heart so close to mine
And just stay here in this moment
For all the rest of time
Yeah, yeah, yeah, yeah, yeah'

RORY: Stop, just stop.

JACOB: Everyone needs to stop. This has gone way too far!

RORY: Jacob, what did I say?

JACOB: Sit down and shut up!

RORY: Daddy?

JACOB: This is ridiculous! You are all acting like such bratty children. Tom, stop drinking, you clearly have a problem. Kate, stop treating your husband like a doormat you can walk over and both of you work on the problems in your relationship. Rory, stop stirring the pot and maybe you wouldn't be so lonely if you stopped looking for love in saunas and on grinder. Michael, I know you are competitive, but you need grow up and trust me when I tell you I love you. And Shane, I'm sorry you are hurting, but you don't get to walk into my house and treat my fiancé the way you have! We are over and you will never be '*stealing*' me back. And Claire, you have been nothing but horrible to Michael this whole night, I think you and Shane should just go.

CLAIRE: Oh, come off it, Jacob. He's just being a little pussy because he's jealous!

RORY: Oh, my god... pussy... pussy cat... my laptop? You keep bringing it up.

MICHAEL: Of course, I'm jealous! Claire, you brought Jacobs ex-fiancé into our home on the night that we planned to announce our engagement to break us up.

CLAIRE: I don't know what you could be possibly talking about.

MICHAEL: Claire, you brought props and he was practically dry humping Jacob on my little sister's twister mat.

CLAIRE: Your little sisters? Really?

RORY: Ooh, another zinger from Claire!

MICHAEL: Rory!

RORY: It's the poppers. I've got a problem.

MICHAEL: And you sit there and deny it like you are some angel! Ugh, Jacob is right. Claire, get the fuck out of my house... *(turning vocally aggressive)* no you sit the fuck down!

[They all stare at Michael for this uncharacteristic outburst.]

CLAIRE: What?

MICHAEL: I don't know! I'm angry!

CLAIRE: Well...

MICHAEL: *(Turning vocally aggressive again)* You shut your fuck hole and you listen to mine!

[They all stare at Michael for this uncharacteristic outburst.]

CLAIRE: Oh, I can't be dealing with this. You know what, Michael?

[Claire makes a masturbation gesture towards Michael make a squishing sound as she does.]

MICHAEL: Oh, yeah? Well...

[Michael copies her throwing it back at Claire.]

Right back at you.

CLAIRE: Oh, yeah?

MICHAEL: Yeah!

[They continue back in forth until Rory jumps in front of them to stop it but mimes getting semen on his face and in his eye.]

RORY: Stop it, guys! Stop it! *(To Michael)* Look at yourself. *(To Claire)* and look at yourself. Now look at me, I look rather pretty. But back to both of you! You've got imaginary cum all over the place. Who is going to clean this up? Who? You are both so immature.

[Rory walks back to his seat taking a large sniff of his poppers. Silence.]

MICHAEL: *Claire, what have I done that made you hate me so much? Honestly, is it something I've said or done, or is it just me? Am I too up tight, or loud, or camp? 'Cause you know it could be worse - I mean I don't walk around shouting 'yas gurl' or clicking my tongue or, like, I didn't even like that recent *Meghan Trainer* song.

[Everyone gasps.]

KATE: I love that song.

SHANE: You're a monster.

RORY: You're supposed to be white!

MICHAEL: Tell me, Claire, is it something I can change or is it just me because I – I don't... I just... I just don't think I can do it anymore.

JACOB: What are you saying?

MICHAEL: Jacob... Jacob, I'm sorry, I love you, but if this is how it's going to be every time, we are in a room together, I don't think I can do it. I've tried my best all these years but look at her – look at tonight. She hates me and I'm not gonna be that person that makes you choose between your family or me. I'm just not gonna do it.

JACOB: Michael, wait...

MICHAEL: No, stop. I'm sorry.

[Michael rushes out.]

JACOB: What have you done?

SHANE: Jac...

JACOB: You shut up! Claire start speaking! What is your problem with Michael?

CLAIRE: Jacob, maybe we should talk about this somewhere else.

JACOB: Claire, I mean it start talking. Now!

CLAIRE: He cheated on you!

JACOB: He what? When?

KATE: Michael would never do that!

RORY: Yeah, even when he was a slut he still believed in monogamy.

CLAIRE: Ok, fine he didn't cheat on you! What he did was much worse.

JACOB: What did he do?

CLAIRE: He hit our mum.

JACOB: No, he didn't!

CLAIRE: Ok, fine he didn't hit her.

RORY: I might hit her for giving birth to you two whiny bitches.

KATE: Get in line.

TOM: There are a few mothers you'd like to hit aren't there?

KATE: *(Whispers)* Fuck your mother!

JACOB: Claire, what did he do?

CLAIRE: He didn't *do* anything.

JACOB: Then what's the problem?

CLAIRE: It's… just *him* in general. I don't know, he's too… *perfect.*

JACOB: What?

RORY: I really thought she was going to go for the camp thing.

KATE: I was thinking that!

JACOB: He's too perfect?

CLAIRE: Yes! Ok! Ever since you introduced him to our family, all he does is talk about how great his life is, with his happily married parents and his fancy house in the countryside with all their beautiful animals and acres and acres of land. Then he struts around with his tailored clothes, talking about his little café that's just doing oh, so well; that it's constantly buzzing! Jacob, he thinks he is better than us! Probably laughing at us growing up in our shitty council estate, having to share a bedroom until the age of eighteen because mum could only afford a one bed flat, and Dad not being in the picture. He's even changing you! Look at this house Jacob this is not you! These pillows? Soap in the bathroom? A snacks platter? And who leaves out dry nuts and fruit at the door for guests?

JACOB: You mean the potpourri?

TOM: It was delicious by the way.

CLAIRE: Look at that! Using all these fancy words with your weird friends and monthly game nights – I mean who the fuck has game nights these days? Just play spin the needle like a normal Londoner!

[Michael Enters.]

MICHAEL: Is that really what you think Claire?

CLAIRE: Michael, I didn't know you were…

MICHAEL: Eavesdropping? Oh, please I'm gay - I'm not gonna have a dramatic tear-filled monologue and then storm out without sticking around to see how people react to it.

RORY: It's true, we do do that.

JACOB: Yeah.

SHANE: He's got a point.

MICHAEL: You really think I'm too perfect? Claire, you couldn't be more wrong! Ask Rory if you don't believe me! My mum and dad, they hate each other they, just refuse to get a divorce because they are super religious which, guess what? It means they aren't too keen on me and my 'lifestyle', either. Since you've known me, how often have I gone back home to visit? I fucking hate that place! Do you know what it was like growing up in a tiny Irish village in the nineties, with all the gossiping neighbours knowing every movement you'd make? And that beautiful farm with all the frolicking animals you imagine? Have you ever been to a real farm? Farms smell like shit twenty-four-seven… like seriously. You wash and you wash, and you wash and still… shit. The worst thing about it is people back there don't even smell it, that's their smell. They like it!

And those cute animals? Yeah, ok, you play with them every day, but then suddenly after your mum feeds you dinner you realise fluffy the family sheep is missing.

KATE: Oh, my god! You ate fluffy!

MICHAEL: As for my café? When have I ever said it was buzzing? Look at that snack's platter, right there is my last attempt at salvaging that 'buzzing café' you think I own. It's about to go bankrupt.

JACOB: *(Looking nervous)* What?

MICHAEL: Shh, sweetie, it's not important right now. Claire, I'll give you the clothes dig, but I only dress well so I can look good and seem sane because the gays in this city have this awful need to appear perfect but- ugh... I'm a mess. I'm a big fucking mess. The only thing I have going even slightly well for me is your brother.

[Silence.]

CLAIRE: Oh, Michael, I don't know what to say. I'm sorry, I didn't realise your life was so pathetic.

MICHAEL: It is.

CLAIRE: Like, really pathetic.

MICHAEL: Really, really pathetic.

RORY: Really, really, really pathetic.

MICHAEL: Ok, we get it!

CLAIRE: No, but I mean It. Me and Jacob didn't have it easy growing up, so I guess I just assumed you thought you were better than us. But you're so pathetic.

RORY: So, so, so pathetic.

MICHAEL: Enough! I'm sorry I ever gave you that impression Claire, I was only ever trying to impress you, but I know I can be a bit much.

RORY: It's true, he is.

JACOB: Yeah.

KATE: He's got a point.

CLAIRE: No, it's my fault, I was too quick to judge. I also think I was afraid of losing Jacob to you. But wait, what's your excuse for this gay house.

MICHAEL: I didn't decorate a single room in this house.

JACOB: I like nice things!

CLAIRE: Oh, my big brother and his pathetic mess of a fiancé. I'm so happy for you!

[Claire forcefully pulls them into an awkward hug. Shane stands up feeling now very awkward.]

SHANE: So, I'm gonna go.

JACOB: No, wait, Shane! I owe you an apology as well. I shouldn't have said all that stuff, I was just angry, and you came in here expecting something else. I'm sorry you had to find out this way.

SHANE: Don't worry, I get it, and for what it's worth you seem really happy. And Michael, I'm really sorry for everything I said earlier, I was just caught up in the drama.

MICHAEL: Shane, I guess I should apologise, too – although amateur porn stars are really popular these days, so really it wasn't an insult. But I am sorry, why don't you stay, it's going to be impossible to get home in this weather and the guest room is already set up anyway.

RORY: That reminds me, guys, it's like torrential snow out there and I left your sunroof wide open.

SHANE: Are you sure?

MICHAEL: Not at all, but you're already here so let's make the most of it, and if you even look in Jacob's direction, I have three knives hidden on my body right now.

RORY: Well, all of that was the gayest thing I've ever seen, and I've watched all of the gay porn out there, literally all of it. I'm in the Guinness book of world records. Look me up. But I guess that's all the drama done for the night.

TOM: *(Trying to joke)* Unless someone wants a threesome?

[Silence.]

KATE: Seriously?

CLAIRE: Wow.

JACOB: Not a good idea.

MICHAEL: It's like you want to die.

TOM: No but – I – It was just a –

SHANE: I don't know you and even I think that was the dumbest thing you've ever said.

RORY: You're a cunt!

KATE: Is that what this is to you, Tom? A joke? Just a big laugh at my expense?

TOM: No! Ah, look why don't we put this on the shelf, eh?

JACOB: That's our thing!

MICHAEL: Yeah!

[Kate glares at them.]

JACOB: But you can borrow it if you want.

MICHAEL: Yeah?

TOM: No, I was just trying to lighten the mood, sweetie. Look, this whole threesome thing has been blown way out of proportion.

KATE: Oh, sorry was three people more than you had in mind? How about you bring some girl home and I'll just stay in the kitchen. So, when I'm filling the dishwasher in there you can be filling her in our bed!

SHANE: How about we all take a moment and...

KATE: Shut your sexy perfect mouth. Jesus it's perfect.

CLAIRE: Ok stop it, before I drip all over the Living room floor.

MICHAEL: I'm not ok with that.

CLAIRE: What the hell happened before you guys got here tonight?

RORY: **Melissa McCarthy does ask a good question.*

[Claire takes a second to acknowledge what he just said]

CLAIRE: Start at the beginning how did this whole threesome thing come about?

KATE: Well, I was deciding what to wear for tonight.

RORY: And you chose that?

KATE: And Tom was in the other room watching TV. He had seemed off for a few days, so I felt a little awkward around the house. So, I wanted to find something sexy to wear to impress him.

RORY: So, you chose that?

KATE: Anyway! I put on my red lace body suit.

CLAIRE: Fuck, yes! *(Eyes now closed getting turned on by the idea)*.

KATE: It's the one I wore on our wedding night; its Tom's favourite...

CLAIRE: What does it look like?

KATE: Ah, well it's like a dark red strapless suit with cut-outs around the waist? Tom said he likes the colour, and it always makes him so...

CLAIRE: *(Turned on)* Back to the body suit! I mean back to the story.

KATE: Well, I thought we would have time to well, y'know, before we had to leave, so put it on and got myself all sexy – you know, the red lip, the heels. Anyway, I went into the living room and came up behind him on the sofa. I started kissing his neck and that's when he stopped me.

CLAIRE: Why would you stop her?! *(Realising her outburst.)* I mean why Tom? What where your reasons for this?

JACOB: I don't think I like you like this.

SHANE: Maybe he is gay?

RORY: Hah! You owe me a fiver!

[Michael angrily gives him a five-pound note. Slowly Jacob also gets up to give him a five-pound note. Eventually even Kate gives him a note.]

TOM: I'm not gay!

[Rory begrudgingly gives them back.]

Look I get that that sounds weird, but you don't know the full story! About a week before that I got home from work early and you were in the kitchen on the phone to your sister. You didn't hear me come in, so I was going to sneak up and scare you. When I got to the kitchen door, I could tell you seemed annoyed, so I decided scaring you was a bad Idea, that's when I heard it.

JACOB: Heard what?

RORY: *(Gasps)* a ghost?

[They all stare at Rory]

TOM: No, I heard you tell Lindsay that you weren't happy, that 'he' isn't enough for you anymore and that you thought you wanted something else. Kate, I panicked. I started thinking of how I could make things better, then when we had sex that weekend you seemed so bored and it hit me, it was the sex! I wasn't satisfying you sexually.

CLAIRE: I would.

TOM: So, even though I hated the idea I thought maybe a threesome with someone you were more attracted to could help or something. I don't know what I was thinking, I just didn't want to lose you.

KATE: Oh, my god.

RORY: What a backstabbing bitch!

KATE: No, I –

CLAIRE: Can you actually not use that phrase? I had a lover who was stabbed in the back when climbing Mount Rushmore.

RORY: Yeah, and my cousin drowned but you don't see me getting upset every time you have a glass of water.

KATE: Guys, its honestly not what you think! Tom, I wasn't talking about you.

TOM: Then who?

RORY: *(Gasps)* The ghost?

[They all stare at Rory.]

MICHAEL: Stop with the poppers!

TOM: Wait, if it's not me then who? Is there another guy?

RORY: So, you're a cheating bitch!

CLAIRE: Can you not use that phrase either? Someone once called me that when I was cheating on them.

RORY: Well, didn't you deserve it, then?

CLAIRE: Yes, but then he mysteriously got stabbed in the back whilst climbing Mount Rushmore.

JACOB: Does mum know you are like this?

KATE: Tom, no! I'm so sorry! Look when I said *he* wasn't enough for me I was talking about Gizmo.

CLAIRE: Who's Gizmo?

MICHAEL: *(Confused)* Their cat?

RORY: Here we go.

KATE: We got gizmo a year ago because we thought we were too young to have a baby. We wanted to see how well we could look after a living thing, and I don't know, lately... lately, I've realised it's not enough. When I said I wanted something else, I meant a baby. Tom, I want to have a baby.

TOM: You do?

KATE: Yes, I know we said we would wait until we got a bigger place, but I think we are ready! I mean, we've done a great job with Gizmo, so I really think we can do this, but... I don't know, what do you think?

TOM: Of course, I want to have a baby!

[They embrace and kiss.]

KATE: I'm so sorry I made you think I wasn't happy. I just can't believe you were going to have a threesome just for me. What would you have done if I brought some guy home?

TOM: I would have done it… for you.

[They all pass Rory the fivers again.]

Kate, I'd do anything for you, I know I don't show it very well, but you mean everything to me.

[Tom finally reveals his whiteboard that has all the correct answers on it. They kiss]

MICHAEL: Wait, I thought you said he was shooting blanks?

KATE: Oh yeah, he annoyed me that day, so I just paid the doctor to say that.

TOM: What?

MICHAEL: Ok, should we try this again and open the other bottle of champagne?

ALL: Yes!

[Michael goes to get the champagne as everyone stands up with their glasses. Jacob pops the cork and fills everyone's glass.]

SHANE: To Michael and Jacob on their engagement.

[They all go to drink.]

JACOB: And to Tom and Kate who are trying to conceive.

[They all go to drink.]

CLAIRE: And to Michael on his amazing platter, I think it will be a hit at the café.

[They all go to drink.]

MICHAEL: And to Claire for –

RORY: Can we just drink?

[They all go to drink.]

KATE: And to –

RORY: Oh, come on!

KATE: And to Rory, the proud new owner of Gizmo the cat. If we are going to be having a baby, we can't have a cat running around causing problems. Happy Birthday!

RORY: *(Teary eyed)* Thank you… To Me!

[They all drink. It turns quiet and slightly uncomfortable as no-one has anything else left to talk about.]

RORY: So, that was like an hour and a half of the night?

SHANE: Wanna have sex?

RORY: So forward. I'm already lubed.

[Rory jumps into Shane's arms and they rush out.]

CLAIRE: Can you believe I was gonna try have a threesome with you guys?

KATE: I know, it's crazy, right?

TOM: So crazy.

CLAIRE: I knew you guys were too good, though.

KATE: What do you mean *'too good'*?

CLAIRE: Well, you just don't seem like the threesome type that's all.

TOM: We get kinky.

KATE: Yeah! They used to call me kinky Kate.

MICHAEL: No one ever called you that.

CLAIRE: Look, I didn't mean to offend, and it doesn't matter cause with you guys wanting to have a baby I guess those days are behind you now?

KATE: Yes, well I guess so.

TOM: I guess so.

KATE: Goodbye!

TOM: Behind us.

KATE: Gone.

TOM: Good riddance.

KATE: Adios.

TOM: Don't miss them days at all.

KATE: Not. At. All.

TOM: Bored of them, actually.

KATE: Boring.

TOM: Snooze fest!

KATE: Yawn.

TOM: Never again.

KATE: Not. Even. Once.

[Silence.]

CLAIRE: So where are we doing this?

BOTH: Michael and Jacobs bed?

[The three of them jump to their feet.]

KATE: I fucking loved when you pissed on me.

CLAIRE: I love getting pissed on.

[The three of them rush out.]

MICHAEL: Well, this wasn't really the engagement party I expected.

JACOB: Oh, really? My ex-fiancé having sex with your cousin and my sister having a threesome in my bed is exactly what I expected!

MICHAEL: *(Raising his glass)* To us?

JACOB: May we never get as crazy as our friends and family.

MICHAEL: You know, our bedroom and the guest room may not be free, but Rory did leave his poppers behind.

JACOB: What are you thinking?

MICHAEL: Oh, I don't know. We could maybe run a bath, light some candles, use some poppers?

JACOB: Oh?

MICHAEL: It could be like that time in Italy when we didn't leave the hotel room?

JACOB: That wasn't me. That was you and your ex.

[Michael freezes realising his mistake.]

MICHAEL: How about we put it on the shelf?

[Michael runs out and Jacob chases him.]

END